MAYBE, PROBABLY

SAISHA BHARGAV

It is easy to be beautiful; it is difficult to appear so. I admire you, beloved, for the trap you've set. It's like a final chapter no one reads because the plot is over.

Frank O'Hara

Contents

Foreword *vii*

Preface *ix*

INT. Last Weeks Of October

October And It's Colours.

1. Can I Sit With You? 5
2. Lunch For One, Please 7
3. Walk With Me? 8
4. Secrets In The Air 10
5. Lonely City 12

End.

Act 1 : Beginning Of An End

6. January Is Here 17
7. Does It Feel Sad Or Loved? 18
8. Maybe I Am Thinking Too Much 19
9. How To Say What You Want? 20
10. Cheers, To Love. 21

End.

Act 2: Somewhere Along The Way, We Changed.

11. That One Woman With Red Hair, Drinking Coffee 27
12. That One Man With Glasses, And A Kind Face 29
13. That One Man, With A Smile On His Face 30

End.

Act 3: Only Love Is All Maroon

14. Isn't The Moon Beautiful Tonight? 35

Contents

15. Can You Stay, Maybe? 37

16. Maybe It's Time... 38

Probably Next Winter.

Fade To Black.

Acknowledgements 43

Notes 45

Foreword

Preface

This book is written in parts, reflecting upon the stages every poem went through. The book follows frequent conversations between a said person with themselves or others, mostly indirectly. This person walks through seasons, feeling and figuring out what they think about the world, people, and especially- love.

This is a work of fiction and in no way romanticizes mental health. Some parts may be troubling for some readers, or not, but please do be mindful. This book is a personal project and is written with the hope to bring comfort to people who are going through tough times.

*it is advisable to read the *Acts* together, as they are divided.

INT. Last weeks of October

October and it's colours.

1. Can i sit with you?

October feels like the warmth of the sun in the early hours of a winter morning,
it feels like the ice water on a hot summer day,
it is composed of an unfinished love story,
and the ending of a coming-of-age movie;
I don't know if it is beautiful, but an unsaid goodbye
with a lingering gaze carries a string of words, more than a goodbye can sing
and it is composed of the unfinished kisses between you and me-
which has no beginning or an end.
October reminds me of the fragrance of *harshringar*
It reminds me of our love and our losses,
It takes me back to the nights-
when I walked under this tree,
I wonder if it still stands in that alley,
If someone else passes by and thinks of their life like me.
Last year, this time, I read a book that tore my heart,
I watched a movie that took me back to my childhood,
it left me wondering -
if I could steal the essence of the story to make it mine-
I wonder now if my story could carry the same fragrance,
Of *harshringar,* between the pages,

in the spine,
all year long,
If it could, maybe, carry all my love for you, and *if* it could live
between the branches of this tree.
Maybe next year this time,
we both must've forgotten what our love consisted of,
but if one October night we walk past a *harshringar* tree,
just know that our love still lives somewhere along those branches.

2. Lunch for one, please

I long for the feeling-
the feeling of home,
the feeling of a warm dinner,
with days getting shorter,
evening comes up early;
It's getting cold all around me,
And the warmth of my hands
is slowly dissipating
I long to sit in my bed
slowly falling into a slumber
grey murmur of the music
Slowly builds a temporary home this winter
In my heart
And it stays with me through days and nights
Maybe this winter will wash away
Like the teardrops clinging onto your eyes
Slowly and quietly,
This winter will tun into mist
In a couple of months
And I will wait for winter to come along once again.

3. Walk with me?

"What would strangeness feel like",
You'd ask and I'd tell you some poetic lines to make you feel warm;
That strangeness felt like the empty page with a blot of ink smeared across
and it colors you with the feeling of blue,
brushing of fingers on the familiar broken walls of your house that made you sigh,
the spaces between your fingers are now painted
with the unfamiliarity of loneliness creeping all the way to your eyes.
Strangeness felt like the silence,
after a song ends and the buzzing of lights during the winter nights.
But, this is all a sugarcoated version of what strangeness feels like.
It breaks you and builds you high and then brings you down.
Strangeness feels cryptic that makes you numb,
and it feels like the drop of your heart in your stomach,
thousands of people looking at you when no one even notices you.
It is *not* pink-hued clouds with a silver lining,
it's dark and it's dense,

and as you stand here you feel that even if the tectonic plates move,
it wouldn't be a tragedy.

4. Secrets in the air

We stand under a tree,
side by side- with our hands so loosely intertwined.
I look at you and you look at me.
We don't say a word.
We look at each other and our hands find their way
back to each other's backs and i lean on your shoulder.
You were here and I was here.
The sounds of the waves crashing,
birds finding their way back to each other.
I hope they find a home.
You are here and I am here, breathing close.
If this isn't happiness, what is?
What else could I ask for?
I find a piece of stick which makes you laugh,
and you ask me-if i will make a heart and write your name?
I wanted to but what if the waves erase your name?
I laugh and throw it away.
The birds settled on the rocks,
the misty air, the crashing waves
and you murmuring *Bon Iver-*
it's intoxicating.
The trees sway above us,
broken boats kept on top of each other.

We don't say a word but our hands have a conversation of their own.
How are you the way you are?

5. Lonely City

The city is floating tonight,
In the dreams and tears of us,
How *still* the building stands, and
how frail are the people standing in them?
This city tonight echoes the words of *Ghalib*,
if you slow down,
you might just catch the music,
of people singing tonight.
This music, i long for,
is the music of people,
of love and of the ones who are watching this,
The ocean this city *is* tonight and
some diving deep to reminisce the ones they lost.
This city tonight,
holds the secrets of me and you,
let's visit every night and stand in this ocean,
one night we might just sigh in relief
and join the harmony of music this night plays.

End.

Act 1 : Beginning of an end

6. January is here

I sit here again tonight,
finding the right words to explain the feeling of love.
But I ask myself, *have I ever felt the feeling of love?*
Maybe the fleeting moments of love,
like the first time, a boy said he loved me.
But it wasn't love entirely.
Maybe when I saw my friend again after years of separation.
Or maybe when I find myself walking at night,
in the winters of January,
and the grass is damp from the cold,
and at a distance,
they shine.
And i see the tree,
that was dying a few months ago,
is bearing the January cold.

7. Does it feel sad or loved?

But love isn't for me.
It's a feeling,
that I tend to look for,
When I have just ceased to feel sadness.
And I wish to feel something else.
It's a selfish thing to do,
but I find myself looking for sadness
In the very thing in front of me.
Like this pen,
or diary.
How weary must they be while bearing the thoughts of myself?
When they get buried in my bag
In an attempt to not feel alone
and the act of keeping this diary makes me happy,
does it feel sad or loved?

8. Maybe I am thinking too much

Sometimes when I sit in my bed,
I feel this hollowness of somebody sitting beside me.
It looks like me by the outline
But, inside, there's nothing.
And sometimes I feel that's me.
Earlier, I waited for sadness to leave,
but now I wait for it to sit beside me
And become the narrator of my story,
Because I am only good at narrating sadness,
that sits beside me.
It's a twofold system of trust.
Sometimes it fails,
But occasionally it allows me to uncover
the truth of my beliefs.

9. How to say what you want?

At times, when I stand and
watch the people wandering in the distance,
cars hurrying by,
dogs napping on the road,
and I see the woman watering the tulsi plant
in the mandir,
that mere act is more peaceful than any night of sleep.
I wonder why Sufi's whirl,
their hands up in the air,
dancing to the music of the universe,
But when I watch that sheer act,
I feel that's what you do in love.
You let yourself *go*,
you exist in every particle
in this universe for this person,
who stands in front of you,
And has taken refuge in your heart,
and you let yourself just be.

10. Cheers, to love.

But this isn't for love,
it's not even for sadness,
this is for that feeling in between.
When I watch the moon on a misty, cold night,
I hope for happiness,
but maybe it's there,
and I'm standing selfish,
because being capable to watch this moon,
in the sky tonight,
being the star of the show,
is happiness.
But, there is sadness lingering over the outlines of the moon,
This *sadness,*
It lies in watching someone you love,
dissipate into silence,
it orbits between the last calls of that one
and it is in the final line of the song,
when you close your eyes
and stand in the middle of this room,
you are dancing to the music playing in your ears,
and you brush your fingers to your face,
you feel yourself tearing up,
but you don't feel hurt,

it is in the light dipping into your room,
for a brief moment,
and you hear the end of the song building up,
And then it unites with a broken sigh from you.

End.

Act 2: Somewhere along the way, we changed.

11. That one woman with red hair, drinking coffee

I sit in this room tonight,
People around me sit in loneliness
standing on their shoulders,
their happiness lingering on the fingertips,
as they hold onto the warm mugs,
sipping hope.
Tonight we talk about winters.
There's a woman sitting in front of me,
holding a worn-out book of poems,
so dearly as if it holds her life,
her love,
and her whole self,
there's a shawl draped over her shoulders,
as if she is unknowingly asking to be comforted.
But her smile is what gives her sadness away,
she opens her book and reads out a poem
about how life has never brought her a drink,
How she sits alone in the restaurant
and drinks the night away,
how every day she does what she hates,
how there is no one waiting for her to be back home,
How the seasons change but, life,

it never comes to sit with her,
but she still waits for life to buy her a drink.

12. That one man with glasses, and a kind face

There's a man sitting beside me,
smelling of musk perfume,
He goes to the office every day
and works till the evening,
But while he is on the way home, he thinks,
how his days turn into nights and
turn into years and his life passes by
as he stands in the traffic,
But he sits with us,
with a smile as warm as the lights shining outside the window,
upon the tree of the red bougainvillea.
Two girls, of the same age, sit together,
One bickers with the other,
One tries to sing about winters,
one tries to tell a story about winters,
The adult shushes them,
        like the full moon sits silently in the night outside.

13. That one man, with a smile on his face

A kid wearing a red sweatshirt brings a tray of roasted peanuts,
he has the biggest smile on his face,
as if he is the richest person on this planet,
and maybe he is.
There's an old man sitting in the corner of the room,
smiling silently whenever the kids bicker with each other,
he sits there with patience beaming all around him,
It was supposed to be an ordinary day,
It was supposed to be a silent night,
But as I sit here,
and I listen to these people talk about life
and love on this winter night,
Maybe life can sometimes surprise you,
It can bring you a warm cup of coffee,
some roasted peanuts,
and *hope* that exists between these pages of books
that surrounds me,
among the people that sit together.
The laughter hides the pain in this room tonight,
darkness sits behind the light,
We are all different, living different lives and loving differently,
But tonight, this warmth on a cold night brings us all together.

End.

Act 3: Only love is all maroon

14. Isn't the moon beautiful tonight?

I love you here
with the present,
with my skin that holds me,
between my teeth,
with every breath that leaves my body,
I love you here,
Where the world starts to think about love,
between the evening that is colored purple,
and the sun that paints my windows yellow,
and where the world forgets about love,
I love you here,
When I am losing the confidence to get myself out of bed,
for a hand to hold my head and save me from myself.
I love you here,
With my self evaporating slowly,
and steadily in the sky of this fast-paced world,
But I love you slowly,
Lying under the shadow of this tree,
overlooking the graveyard of my heart,
slowly as this ladybug tries to get past the fallen leaves,
as the older couple falls in love with each other every evening,
as the bench in this park waits through four seasons,

Wishing, that by tomorrow you'll love me too.

15. Can you stay, maybe?

After a tiring summer,
I find you again
between this frosty air,
and the dark clouds;
I long for you,
as the plant in the corner of my room,
for a ray of sunlight.
Till then I am warming my heart
with the sound of this rustic radio you left.
It's cold now,
How long till I see you,
hear you, whisper away,
warm nothings?
After a long night, I forget you
And fill the back of my car with all that you left me;
enough for a lifetime of winters.
I'll sit in front of the bonfire and
watch the memories of you burn away.
The snow falls on my face and,
it melts away soon, and I'd like for it to stay,
But you can't ask something to stay,
If its sole purpose is to leave.

16. Maybe it's time...

More often than not,
I imagine sitting *here*,
beside this window that overlooks the busy road,
i imagine you sitting across from me,
and when I am having a hard day,
imagining you makes the day pass in a daze.
Today, I play a role of a person *who is loved*,
I walk the streets crowded with people thinking I am loved,
And I love someone *enough*,
Mabe when I pick up some flowers for my room,
I am doing so because I am loved.
When I stand in the balcony tonight,
and it is cold and quiet,
and the only sound I hear;
is of the rain falling.
It is so quiet that I can hear my breathing,
And to know I am loved,
Is the greatest pleasure.
And when I am eating the food tonight,
The small task of feeding myself becomes *beautiful*
Because at that moment,
I am loved,
and everything around me turns to life.

Probably next winter.

Fade to black.

Acknowledgements

This book has been a long-awaited challenge for me, but it has been possible because of some people. This page is for anyone who has believed in me. My brother, my mother- for always, always encouraging me to write, and do this.

For my friends- I am *so* lucky to have you all. Thank you for doing so. This has been possible because of you.

Never would i have believed in the past that one day I would be writing this page here right now. I love words, and the feeling they bring with them. And I hope *you* who is probably reading this, feels that way.

Notes

- Forever grateful to Frank O'Hara for existing and his works.
- Act 3 title taken from Bon Iver- Only love is all maroon.
- In poem 11. reference to a poem "a glass of drink" by Jeong Ho Seung.

9 798887 722023

Printed by Libri Plureos GmbH in Hamburg,
Germany